POWERFUL
Place Value

Lisa Arias

Educational Media

rourkeeducationalmedia.com

Before Reading:

Building Academic Vocabulary and Background Knowledge

Before reading a book, it is important to tap into what your child or students already know about the topic. This will help them develop their vocabulary, increase their reading comprehension, and make connections across the curriculum.

1. *Look at the cover of the book. What will this book be about?*
2. *What do you already know about the topic?*
3. *Let's study the Table of Contents. What will you learn about in the book's chapters?*
4. *What would you like to learn about this topic? Do you think you might learn about it from this book? Why or why not?*
5. *Use a reading journal to write about your knowledge of this topic. Record what you already know about the topic and what you hope to learn about the topic.*
6. *Read the book.*
7. *In your reading journal, record what you learned about the topic and your response to the book.*
8. *After reading the book complete the activities below.*

Content Area Vocabulary
Read the list. What do these words mean?

base ten blocks
digits
expanded notation
infinity
period
place value
short word form
standard form
sum
whole numbers
word form

After Reading:

Comprehension and Extension Activity

After reading the book, work on the following questions with your child or students in order to check their level of reading comprehension and content mastery.

1. *If a number contained a zero in it, would you include it in expanded notation? Why? (Asking questions)*
2. *How are place values converted? (Summarize)*
3. *Why are zeros never said in numbers such as 100 or 1,050? (Asking questions)*
4. *Why are commas used in number and word form? (Summarize)*
5. *How does expanded notation help you better understand a number? (Asking questions)*

Extension Activity

Choose any 6-digit number. Write the number at the top of a piece of paper. Don't forget the commas! Underneath the number write it in word form and short word form. On another section of the paper, draw out the number using base ten blocks or a base ten chart. In a different area of the paper, write out the number using expanded notation. How many different ways did you write your number? Explain the benefit of each.

Table of Contents

Letters and Digits

Counting with numbers is how it is done.
Time to begin with some **place value** fun!

Letters make words.

Digits make numbers.

Place Value

It is really true, every digit has a place value!

Each value is hidden and depends on the digit's position.

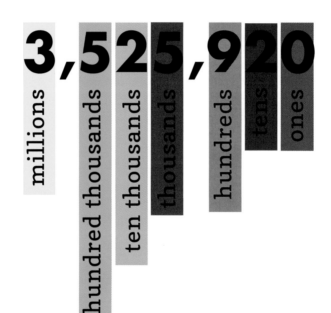

3,525,920

millions | hundred thousands | ten thousands | thousands | hundreds | tens | ones

Check It Out!

In large numbers, every three digits are separated with a comma, but each group is called a **period**.

Name the place value position for each highlighted digit.

0

20

920

5,920

25,920

525,920

3,525,920

Standard Form

Numbers in **standard form** group digits in sets of three.
This helps keep track of place value for you and me.

Look closely and you will see
how commas separate each group perfectly.

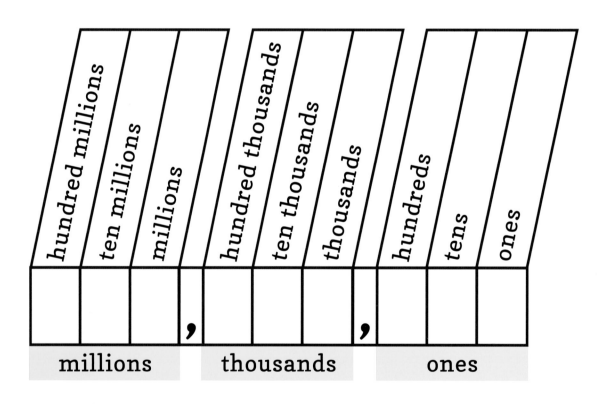

Believe it or not, these groups of three
go on for **infinity**.

Numbers are so clever,
infinity lets you count on forever.

infinity sign

You can count by ones, tens, hundreds, thousands, millions, billions,
trillions, quadrillions, quintillions, sextillions, octillions, and even
more thanks to infinity!

Read Numbers

When you have a large number, look at each group separately. Then, read aloud the first group of three.

The place value for each group is said when the next comma is read.

146,298

One hundred forty-six

Thousand

Two hundred ninety-eight

Always say the number you see,
no matter how many digits are in the first group of three.

12,240,546

Twelve

Million

Two hundred forty

Thousand

Five hundred forty-six

When a number is read,
the digit zero is never said.

A zero's job is key to filling unused spaces in each group of three.

2,000,000

Two

Million

25,001

Twenty-five

Thousand

One

Check It Out!

When reading **whole numbers**, the word
"and" is always banned.

Say each number.

1,931
one thousand, nine hundred thirty-one

3,016
three thousand, sixteen

43,041
forty-three thousand, forty-one

15,012
fifteen thousand, twelve

5,088,776
five million, eighty-eight thousand,
seven hundred seventy-six

3,519,994
three million, five hundred nineteen
thousand, nine hundred ninety-four

Word Form

Writing numbers in **word form** may take a little time. Use words instead of numbers and you will be just fine.

For numbers up to twenty, just write the word exactly how the number is heard.

EIGHT	SEVEN
EIGHTEEN	SEVENTEEN
ELEVEN	SIX
FIFTEEN	SIXTEEN
FIVE	TEN
FOUR	THIRTEEN
FOURTEEN	THREE
NINE	TWELVE
NINETEEN	TWENTY
ONE	TWO

A	G	I	T	Y	N	E	L	W	Q	C	N	L	B	M
U	E	C	S	S	T	H	I	R	T	E	E	N	F	K
J	S	B	W	E	V	Y	N	V	E	S	Z	Q	I	F
B	E	Z	H	N	I	N	E	T	E	E	N	Y	F	O
I	V	T	R	J	V	H	R	Z	W	Q	T	E	T	U
D	E	W	Z	R	S	U	B	G	Z	N	J	I	E	R
H	N	E	C	I	O	E	D	V	E	S	U	G	E	K
R	T	L	K	F	S	K	V	W	O	W	K	H	N	S
I	E	V	E	I	G	H	T	E	E	N	E	T	W	O
H	E	E	H	R	W	X	C	G	N	R	R	P	I	O
T	N	B	F	D	W	O	S	I	X	T	E	E	N	H
H	F	I	V	E	E	N	G	Z	L	I	X	O	V	O
R	T	L	T	N	C	E	T	N	H	I	U	U	D	A
E	J	U	I	N	R	B	E	L	S	X	Q	K	W	T
E	E	N	R	C	N	T	N	E	L	E	V	E	N	K

15

A **hyphen** is used most every time
when writing numbers from 21 through 99.

21

twenty-one

35

thirty-five

43

forty-three

87

eighty-seven

99

ninety-nine

16

Even in word form, a **comma** is used to separate place values.

8,776

eight thousand, seven hundred seventy-six

3,519,994

Three million, five hundred nineteen thousand, nine hundred ninety-four

6,188,114

Six million, one hundred eighty-eight thousand, one hundred fourteen

Short Word Form

Writing numbers in **short word form** is so quick.
Combining words and numbers is the trick.

3,707
3 thousand, 707

865,331
865 thousand, 331

5,088,776

5 million, 88 thousand, 776

445,001

445 thousand, 1

23,980

23 thousand, 980

10,010

10 thousand, 10

Place Value Models

Base ten blocks are an important tool to help model numbers at home and at school.

Each size block is based on the number ten, just like our number system.

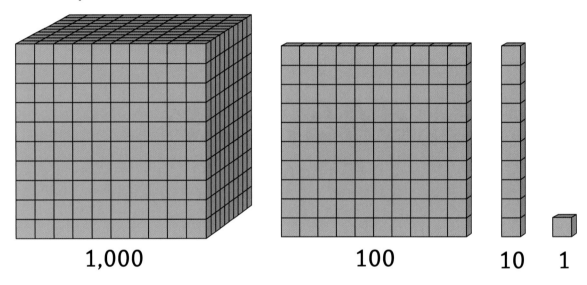

1,000   100   10   1

Check It Out!

Our number system is called base ten because each place value is 10 times more than the value to the right of it.

Create each digit's value with blocks.

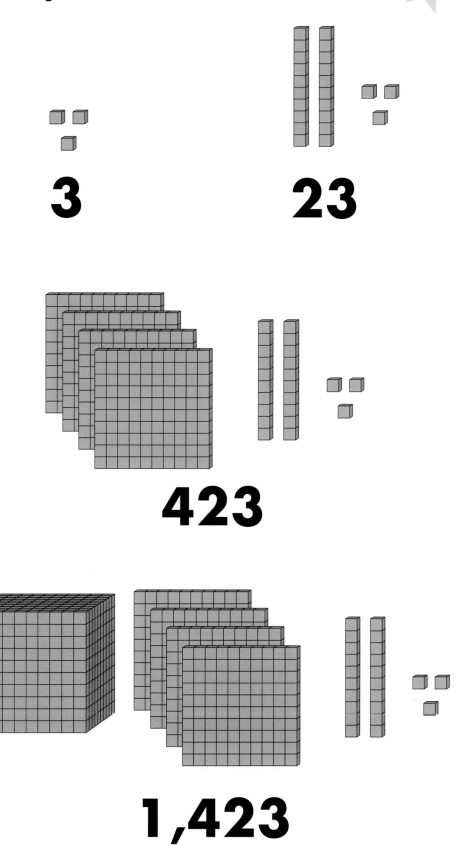

3

23

423

1,423

Find the number for each model.

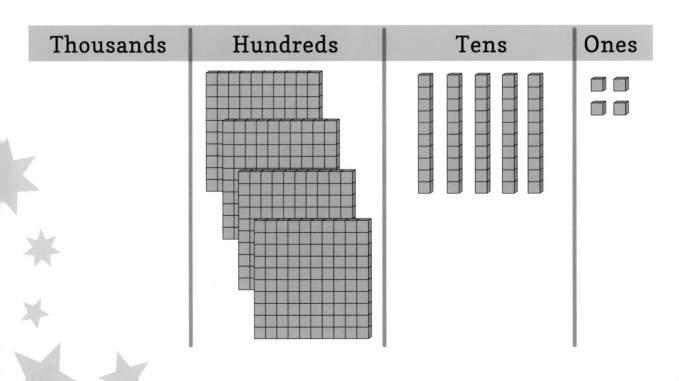

Thousands	Hundreds	Tens	Ones

Thousands	Hundreds	Tens	Ones

Thousands	Hundreds	Tens	Ones

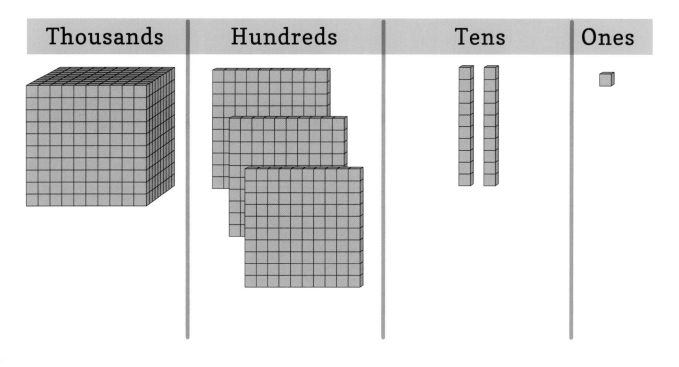

Thousands	Hundreds	Tens	Ones

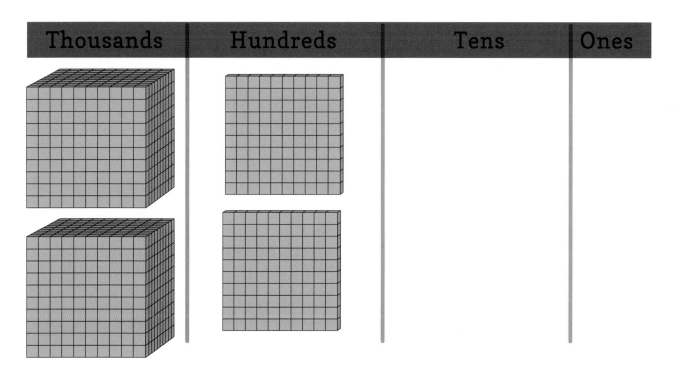

Expanded Notation

Writing numbers in **expanded notation** is really cool.
Find the value of each digit is what you do.

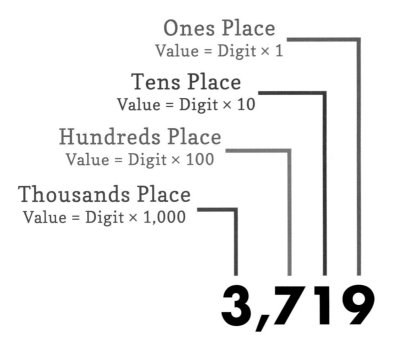

Ones Place
Value = Digit × 1

Tens Place
Value = Digit × 10

Hundreds Place
Value = Digit × 100

Thousands Place
Value = Digit × 1,000

3,719

The **sum** of the digit's value is equal to the number.

3,000 + **7**00 + **1**0 + **9** = 3,719

Say each number in expanded notation.

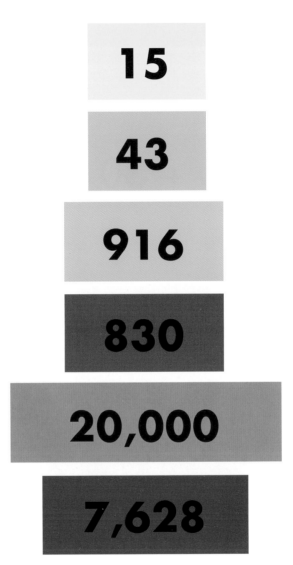

15

43

916

830

20,000

7,628

Time for a celebration! Find the standard form of each number that is written in expanded notation.

500 + 30 + 1

20,000 + 8,000 + 400 + 50 + 3

1,000 + 600 + 20 + 7

Answers:

531

28,453

1,627

619

42

130,700

100,000 + 30,000 + 700

40 + 2

600 + 10 + 9

Converting Place Values

Converting between place values may seem hard to do.
No need to worry. Zero becomes the hero for me and you.

Millions			Thousands			Ones		
Hundred Millions	Ten Millions	Millions	Hundred Thousands	Ten Thousands	Thousands	Hundreds	Tens	Ones

× 10   × 10   × 10   × 10   × 10   × 10   × 10   × 10

Each place value spot is 10 times more than the value to its right.

To convert a place value, use the chart to guide you.
Add zeros on the chart from the value you have to the value you want.

How many tens are in 1,000?

Millions			Thousands			Ones		
Hundred Millions	Ten Millions	Millions	Hundred Thousands	Ten Thousands	Thousands	Hundreds	Tens	Ones
					1	0	0	

How many tens are in 3,000?

Millions			Thousands			Ones		
Hundred Millions	Ten Millions	Millions	Hundred Thousands	Ten Thousands	Thousands	Hundreds	Tens	Ones
					3	0	0	

How many hundreds are in 4,000,000?

Millions			Thousands			Ones		
Hundred Millions	Ten Millions	Millions	Hundred Thousands	Ten Thousands	Thousands	Hundreds	Tens	Ones
		4	0	0	0	0		

How many thousands are in 4,000,000?

Millions			Thousands			Ones		
Hundred Millions	Ten Millions	Millions	Hundred Thousands	Ten Thousands	Thousands	Hundreds	Tens	Ones
		4	0	0	0			

How many thousands are in 20,000?

Millions			Thousands			Ones		
Hundred Millions	Ten Millions	Millions	Hundred Thousands	Ten Thousands	Thousands	Hundreds	Tens	Ones
				2	0			

How many tens are in 27, 000?

Millions			Thousands			Ones		
Hundred Millions	Ten Millions	Millions	Hundred Thousands	Ten Thousands	Thousands	Hundreds	Tens	Ones
				2	7	0	0	

Glossary

base ten blocks (BAYSS TEN BLOKS): blocks used to model numbers

digits (DIJ-its): numbers from 0 to 9

expanded notation (ek-SPAN-did noh-TAY-shuhn): a number written in the form of each digit's place value

infinity (in-FIN-i-tee): without end

period (PIHR-ee-ud): each group of three digits in a number

place value (PLAYSS VAL-yoo): the value of each digit of a number based on its position

short word form (SHORT WURD FORM): a number written in the form of words and numbers

standard form (STAN-durd FORM): a number written using the digits 0 to 9

sum (SUHM): the answer to an addition problem

whole numbers (HOLE NUHM-burz): numbers including 0,1, 2, 3 that count on to infinity

word form (WURD FORM): a number written with words

Index

Websites to Visit

www.mathcats.com/explore/reallybignumbers.html

www.aaamath.com/plc21bx2.htm

www.softschools.com/math/place_value/

About the Author

Lisa Arias is a math teacher who lives in Tampa, Florida with her husband and two children. Her out-of-the-box thinking and teaching style guided her toward becoming an author. She enjoys playing board games and spending time with family and friends.

Meet The Author!
www.meetREMauthors.com

www.rourkeeducationalmedia.com

PHOTO CREDITS: Cover: © VasjaKoman; Page 4: © jameslee1; Page 9: © Godruma

Edited by: Jill Sherman

Cover and Interior design by: Tara Raymo

Library of Congress PCN Data

Powerful Place Value: Patterns and Power / Lisa Arias
(Got Math!)
  ISBN 978-1-62717-707-8 (hard cover)
  ISBN 978-1-62717-829-7 (soft cover)
  ISBN 978-1-62717-942-3 (e-Book)
Library of Congress Control Number: 2014935584

Printed in the United States of America, North Mankato, Minnesota

3 1333 04427 3306

Also Available as:

ROURKE'S
e-Books